REVISED First Original Edition

My Truth – 10 Days, 10 Words

© Copyright 2022 by Dwight Hairston Currence

ISBN- 979-8-9871031-0-4

Simply Snowden

Table of Contents

Dedication:

This book is dedicated to the two women of God in my life. The first is an incredible lady, mother, mentor, soloist, author, certified personal trainer, and a great person. She ignited a spark in my soul that stopped growing at age sixteen. It was my spiritual growth. I feel sixteen again, and for that, I'm forever grateful.

The second is the woman who feeds my soul daily with humility, walking with God and unconditional love. My daughter, Latoya, is my affirmation that there is a shift in the atmosphere. I'm honored to say Latoya inspires me each and every day.

MY TRUTH

---

10 Days   10 Words

I own my past, and this is my journey. I pray my transparency encourages, comforts, and awakens you. This book is my *truth.*

Unless otherwise stated, all the verses from the Bible are taken from the English Standard Version (ESV).

PREFACE

I can explain, define, and describe my dysfunctional childhood and life, and I can blame, give stats, and give a testimonial as to why I did what I did. None of the reasons matter. I'm grateful for my spiritual awakening today. It's not hard being a Christian; it's hard for me not to be and act like a Christian. My accomplishments were measured by material things before Christ, and I was ego-driven and coward-tough.

As I wrote this book, my experiences seem to be from ages ago. My truth enlightens and humbles me, to be honest and dig deep to remember. My life today stands still because I wake up excited and go to bed with inner peace. Exposing my truth to the world is frightening, but the feeling is invigorating. I didn't know who I was supposed to be because of the person I had become. I had developed into someone I thought must please others because I never felt pleased. I was never happy because I didn't know who I was. I stopped growing mentally at age sixteen. It's going to take another book to explain that.

...Trust me!

I want this book to give you permission to dream. To dream, you must be free. To be free, you must have inner peace. To have inner peace, you must have faith. In order to have faith, you must dream. If that doesn't make sense to you, I hope you take my advice for the next ten days. When you wake up in the morning, the first word that comes to mind, write it down and describe what that word means to you and the feelings and emotions that you feel when you think of that word. During my journey, I wrote about what the word meant to me before Christ and what it meant to me after I gave my life to Christ. If you are on the fence with God, it's okay; no harm, no foul. You will find out what is going on in your mind. This journal will help determine if you are storing resentments in your mind and how they make you feel. I have some words that I woke up with, and I hope you find my journey intriguing.

If you aren't a morning person, write the word down and think about it during the day. Keep a journal because it allows you to look in the mirror as well as a side-view and rearview mirror. I don't have a lot to say because this is about you. You must have conversations with yourself, be honest with yourself, and make all the decisions yourself. I'm just the messenger- Ten days, ten words. That's all.

If you are like me, ten isn't going to be enough, as you can see from my next short read, My Truth - My Journey Continues. Take this journey where you have never been; past your mind, through your heart, to your soul. Who are you really? God doesn't give you a dream without permission to make that dream come true. I was always a writer but not active. Today I am an active writer! Arriving at this place did not come without sacrifice.

THE BEGINNING

My mom got sick and wanted to come to stay with me. I didn't understand that God's plan for my healing was for me to forgive myself. My focus was on my mom, so I didn't have time for a pity party in my mind. Little did I know that I wasn't really taking care of Mom. God had both of us covered. I remember trying to make a deal with God about caring for my mom. I was willing to take care of her, but I didn't want to stop working. God said this is full-time. So, I quit my job on faith. It was the best day of my life thus far. I told God that I trusted Him. I believe that He died and arose. I believe he was alive in me. That was six years ago, on February 14, 2013. In May 2019, I started waking up with words on my mind. In this book. I will introduce you to the words that I journaled about daily. I describe these words and what they meant to me before my relationship with Christ (BC) and then what those words meant to me after I developed a relationship with Christ.

Strap up, and let's go!

Welcome to my journey.

1% is the problem = FEAR

99% is the solution = FAITH

DAY 1 - MARRIAGE

I woke up with the word marriage in my mind. Marriage is a word that I honor today. When people tell me they have been married 20 years, I take a deep breath. I always wanted that to be me. I see old gray-haired couples walking; still holding hands gives me hope. I have been single and dating myself for the past five years. I now understand I was damaged goods in all my marriages. Marriage for me today means more than a ring or piece of paper. It means more than not wanting to be alone. Marriage, for me, today means commitment. Commitment is assurance. How about some more words for commitment; guarantee, promise, or pledge? Marriage is an opportunity to wake up and fall in love all over again every morning. Marriage looks so bright it blinds my eyes.

I now pray for God to guide me to my wife. I believe I don't have any more trust issues. I always had to be in control, and I always had to know the outcome. It reminds me of driving my car. Everything is great when I'm in the driver's seat, and it's a different world on the passenger side. I told God to drive the bus, and it's real-time today.

Check this out!

You must trust someone else in your life. You have no control over the gas or brake pedal. Is that why you are so uncomfortable sitting in the co-pilot seat? Do you tell them how to drive, making them feel like you are still in control? Do you refuse to ride in the co-pilot seat? You must be trustworthy in order to trust.

"Trust in the LORD with all your heart, and do not lean on your own understanding."

Proverbs   3:5

"When I am afraid, I put my trust in you. In God, whose word I praise, in God I trust; I shall not be afraid. What can flesh do to me?"

Psalm   56:3-4

Why do I sometimes feel alone?

Why do I yearn for companionship?

Why do I still want to figure women out?

Why do I want to change them?

Dating sucks, dating sucks, dating sucks! Everything is online now; online dating sucks. Let me tell you about a couple of my dates. The first lady wouldn't look me in the eyes. We went to the mall, and her eyes were all over the place. I believe your eyes are a direct link to your heart. She told me on the second date that she likes men and women. I told her no thank you. The second lady didn't look anything like her picture. Her picture was 15 years younger. She also weighed 150 pounds heavier. There was no way I could trust her. Please, God, take the wheel.

In Genesis 2:18, the LORD God said, "It is not good that the man should be alone; I will make him a helper fit for him."

A helper is defined as a person or thing that gives assistance with support, according to dictionary.com. I do believe assistance with support should come from the husband and wife. The keyword is fit for him, and God made a fit just for you. Don't give up.

Marriage before Christ was a piece of paper that meant she trapped me. I guess I should have looked up the definition of commitment. It doesn't matter. I wasn't ready. I was behaving like a child but wanted to be respected as a man. I always believed they trapped me with a child. They were great women. I never took the time to understand them. I couldn't understand myself. I bled on them daily, and they didn't even cut me. I was cutting myself mentally with the what-if game.

What if we didn't have kids?

Would we still be together?

I just needed someone else to blame, so I didn't have to look at myself in the mirror. I felt obligated to stay for the kids. We didn't have a strong foundation. When my marriages became toxic, I ran. I don't have to run anymore. I'm trembling to remember the baggage I brought into each of my marriages. I pray for all three of my ex-wives to have inner peace. Please forgive me!

DAY 2 - BROTHER AND SISTER

I woke up with the words brother and sister in my mind. It's hard for me to just think about one without the other. My brother and sister keep me grounded. My sister is one year older, and my brother is two years older. Let's start with the word brother. Why does the word brother sound offensive sometimes? It sounds like someone is taking a jab at me. It was painful growing up. I was too light for black people and too dark for white people. I didn't know where I fit in. I look at mixed kids today. I wonder if they have the same struggle I had. I never had a safe place to go in my mind. If I could go back to me as a child, I would say, "God is safety, and he lives." I think it's deeper than the exterior, but it's the exterior. Some words take me down memory lane and have pain and anger attached to them. Okay, back to my brother. My brother was what you would call hard-headed. He would always break the rules. I can remember him having to go outside to get his own switches. (a switch is a small limb off of a tree) I saw him get punished so many times. I didn't want any part of that. He would stand there with marks on his arms and legs without shedding a tear. He would go to the grocery store and make a sandwich. I'm talking about open bread, meat, mayo, and cheese.

Okay, my truth. My brother was in the hospital. I was having some car issues. I borrowed his car. I was backing out of the driveway. I heard the brakes squeak. I told myself it was okay. I got on the highway. There was an accident ahead. I hit the brakes. Oh yeah, they didn't work. I told the police officer I didn't have identification.

My brother got the ticket. When my dad found out, I ran. I can't believe I had no remorse at the time. That was so long ago, but I'm trembling right now.

"A friend loves at all times, and a brother is born for adversity."

Proverbs 17:17

Sister is a word that has had a big impact on my life. Growing up, I isolated myself from my siblings. I would rather hang out in the kitchen and cook with my grandmother. My sister was hit by a black skillet that changed her life forever. I stayed away from her because I didn't want to accept responsibility for her. She had mental issues out of her control. I had anger issues surrounding that horrific night. I isolated myself from her because she was a chain smoker. My sister was hit by a black skillet frying pan. I saw the long line of stitches in her head.

Right here, right now, I get it. I know God has forgiven me. On days like today, It's hard to forgive myself. March 11, 2018, is a day I know my nieces and nephew probably think I don't remember. It was the day my sister passed. I didn't attend the funeral. My truth is I was afraid. I had a hefty dose of *guilt* for not being a part of her life, mixed with *shame* for not being there for my nieces and nephew. This fear sowed seeds of isolation. Still angry from that horrific night. Endless sorrow of the loss of the only person who gave me unconditional love. The negative seeds I was fertilizing had grown knee-high in my mind.

Do you have to have a loss to have a gain?

Did it strengthen my faith at what cost?

I attend funerals today. I know fear and faith don't thrive together. I can't turn back the hands of time. I take ownership of my actions. To my nieces and nephew, please forgive me. To anyone who has a decision to make, don't. Fall on your knees. Pray with your heart. If you let fear grow, my testimony will be yours. I took our relationship away by allowing the enemy to isolate me from the only person who shared most of my story. I was supposed to protect and provide for her. God allows things to happen to good people so people around them can grow their faith in Him. You should enable understanding and not judge them. They are going to get on your nerves. I hope this message saves you from a lesson I learned. It's too late for me to hug my sister, too late to tell her I love her, and too late to ask her does she need anything. My sister is on my eyelids when I feel like giving up. I close my eyes and see her face for inspiration. I know Valerie was always proud of me. She loved me unconditionally. *Failure is not an option.* Rest in peace, Val. Save me a seat between you and Mama Happy.

I look forward to that day.

#FOREVERLIVINGLIFEFALLINGSHORTGETTINGBACKUP!

"But if you do not forgive others their trespasses, neither will your Father forgive your trespasses."

Matthew 6:15

DAY 3 - SEX

I woke up with sex on my mind. It's not a good word for me. I've been celibate for six years. I was talking to my colleagues about my choice one day. I hear at least one joke every week. I don't know why people think it is a form of punishment. It's a lifestyle change. It's a spiritual change. It's caring about my body being a temple.

I went on my first date after being celibate for five years. I was transparent. She took it as a challenge to seduce me. We only had three dates. I had to ghost her. (Ghost means to end communications and disappear.) Ladies, let me drop some knowledge on you. When you buy a car, you see the perfect one; you take it for a test drive. You don't like how it drives, so you continue to test drive cars all day. You come back tomorrow and find the perfect car. Ladies, the only problem is you don't know how many different drivers the car has had. The miles only tell you how far it has been. You are worth the wait—enough of that. I have just a couple of questions.

Do you believe in no sex before marriage?

Would your current relationship last with no sex?

Are you married but bored with sex?

This is my take on it. God must be in the middle of all your relationships. Lust is deceptive, attractive, and satisfying. Lust is the gatekeeper to lure other sins in. Lust wants to control your thoughts.

Lust tells you you need it, but God provides all your needs. Lust confuses you with I deserve it.

I have to stop there!

I explore this in my upcoming book,

MY TRUTH: Seven Deadly Sins Seven Their Heavenly Virtues. It starts with LUST and ends with HUMILITY.

"Flee from sexual immorality. Every other sin a person commits is outside the body, but sexually immoral sins against his own body."

1 Corinthians 6:18

Okay, my truth. I lost my virginity to my teacher in school. They have a word for that today. It's called child molestation. Back in the day, it was called pimping. I'm looking at these words in my journal. How dare Mrs. Child Predator do that to me? She changed my sexual relationship with women. I had developed an alter ego. I turned into stripped-man mode. I only satisfied her and not myself. It was the start of a bad learned behavior of blaming someone else for my happiness. I now believe you are responsible for your own happiness. The people around you are responsible for not taking it away. I didn't know how sick my teenage years were until I started writing in my journal daily. God helped me forgive her. I do wonder if she is still alive.

Sin is attractive because it offers us a quick fix to all your problems. Sin can also make you just blend in. I just went along with the evil, and my appetite became my master. When my desire became my master, I did anything to satisfy it. Sin lures you in with flashy and bright ideas. You can't be friends with sin. Your actions speak louder than words. I told myself many times this was wrong. Sin will try to control your thoughts. Your thoughts will become your actions.

So if you were a victim of molestation, this is the time to forgive yourself. It's not your fault. To properly heal, you must forgive them also. Don't let anyone rent space in your mind for secrets anymore. God protects and covers all those known and unknown of sexual molestation. May they hear your voice and know it is you, God. Feed their faith and chase away the fear in the name of Jesus. Amen.

"Or do you not know that your body is a temple of the Holy Spirit within you, whom you have received from God? You are not your own, for you were bought with a price. So glorify God in your body."

1 Corinthians 6:19-20

DAY 4 - PATIENCE

I woke up with the word patience in my mind. I sometimes think my mind just wanders. Having patience made me think about my tattoos. My little brother does tattoos, and that is a blessing and a curse.

I have four different women's names tattooed on my body. I told them my brother used me for practice. This was another bad decision I made before Christ. I remember the long ride home. I would walk through the door proudly. I would say, I put your name on my body. I hoped they would love me because I didn't want to be alone. Later I found out that wasn't the problem, and the problem was me not loving myself. Today, God is always with me.

What does this have to do with patience?

I want to get them covered up. I'm a Christian, so more ink. I've thought about removing them. Is that cutting on my body?

I'm praying for patience because they now bother me when I look in the mirror.

"But if we hope for what we do not see, we wait for it with patience."

Romans 8:25

I want God to be a microwave, but he decides I need a crockpot. Patience to me means inner peace and freedom in my mind. I know the decision will be the right one, and

I pray for patience every step of the way. My life has changed so much because I let God drive the bus. I don't have to make any decisions. The only decision I make is what I'm going to eat.

What bank do you use with the time you save-always in a hurry? I used to work hard and fast when I was young, and I now spend time planning before I start. It gets me to the same finish line in the same amount of time. I heard this phrase but ignored it. Always work smart, not hard. Get out of your way.

I still struggle with being patient with other people. I had to stop putting expectations on people because it set me up for disappointment. I was taught integrity at a very young age. I have to tell myself, "I don't care." It gives me closure with other people. The more I say it, the more I believe it. I've been told I'm very benevolent. It's not easy walking away. Practice makes perfect. I put the outcome for other people in God's hands. My job is to pray for them, not save them.

"Do not be anxious about anything, but in everything by prayer and supplication with thanksgiving let your requests be made known to God."

Philippians 4:6

DAY 5 - MOM

I woke up thinking about my mom. I remember waiting for her to come to bring our Christmas gifts as a child, and I would blow my breath on the cold window and make smiley faces. The joy turned into anticipation, which turned into heartache, and eventually, crying myself to sleep, thinking that my mom didn't want me. I spent my early years with my grandparents and always felt like my grandmother was my mother. I have a spiritual foundation, structure, and integrity because of my grandparents.

My grandparents always made me feel safe. They were old-fashioned. I can remember the phone call. Mamma Happy had been murdered. I was angry with God for taking her away from me in 1986. I felt like my mom had died. I walked around without a heartbeat. I only had two emotions. They were angry or sad. I was suffering from a hidden state of childhood animation. I made that diagnosis up just now. I went to work. I paid the bills. I cried every moment I was alone.

"Even though I walk, through the valley of the shadow of death, I will fear no evil, for you are with me; your rod and your staff, they comfort me."

Psalm 23:4

I spent my teenage years with my dad. So when my birth mom got sick, I spent some time taking care of her. It turned out to be a blessing. I'm 50 years old and beginning to trust God 100%. I didn't know my mom and I were so much alike. I guess that's why I drove my dad crazy. My mom would look at crying children, and they would stop. I didn't know I got that from her. We both got it from God.

I had one question that I wanted to ask my mom. I wondered why my parents didn't want me. At least, that is the way that I felt. Feeling that way taught me at an early age not to trust, and that created the aimless wandering and loneliness that I had before I found God.

Although I didn't have the guts to ask my mom my one question, she answered it piece by piece as she talked about her past. I felt her pain as she spoke about her life. I couldn't hold back the tears. I thought I had it bad. I not only had closure, but my mom taught me you don't know someone else's story. Don't try to figure them out. Just ask God.

I have a new respect for women taking care of their children. Motherhood is an enormous responsibility. After hearing her stories, I realized the responsibilities were way bigger than I had ever imagined. I am so thankful to have listened to the joy and the pain she felt during her life.

My mom has dementia, and she is a full-time job. I'm grateful she was able to tell me her truth before she got really bad. I feel my mom is living for the first time in my life. She carved out a special place in my heart. I pray for my next wife to act just like my mom. My mom loves the Lord, and so do I.

"My son, keep your father's commandment and forsake not your mother's teaching."

Proverbs 6:20

DAY 6 - PAIN

I woke up with the word pain this morning. I don't know if thinking about my mom all day yesterday put me in this mood. Pain doesn't exist in my life anymore. My pain today is tears of joy. I cry because I am a miracle. It's mind-blowing to look at the word pain and feel satisfied. My walk with God allows me to feel a stranger's pain. I am an elevator inspector, and I had to inspect the elevators at the hospital today. As I met the maintenance guy at the front door, his spirit got to me before him. I felt he was troubled. I don't talk while doing my inspection, as working around elevators is a dangerous job. Once I was done inspecting the elevators, he walked me to the door, and I looked into his eyes. There isn't a word to describe that feeling. We were in the lobby of a busy hospital with people all around us. It's almost like they all disappeared, and I started sharing my story. I told him how God had changed my life. Today, my purpose was confirmed as God took over my thoughts. I felt like a tall lighthouse guiding him in from the fog. We both stood there in the lobby and cried. It's words like pain that don't hurt anymore. I sometimes see the mess, but God sees the miracle.

I want to tell you about the word pain in my past. Maybe you need to hear this. Confrontation requires courage, comfort, and a level of trust. I paid cash for a car in the early 80s. I got the car home and noticed it didn't have a bumper. I tried to return it the same day. I can remember saying to myself, "I'll show him." I drove the car two miles down the road. I set the car on fire. The pain from the confrontation had taken over. I had built walls to isolate myself from myself. You will always have pain when you aren't able to look into your own eyes.

Most of the time, I would let people have their way. I would get angry at myself when I was alone. Most people didn't know I was upset with them. Pain dug me deeper into a shallow grave inside my mind. I only peeked out when the coast was clear. The pain was also what I used to control other people. I used shady hints or jesters to make them feel bad. I used pain as aspirin because that was all I had. I took it morning, noon, and night. My heart was always broken and weak. The sad part is I didn't understand why I did this. This pain I brought on myself became normal. I still feel pain typing these words. I could only imagine how I affected all the people around me. I dare not look into someone's eyes and reveal my secret. They say birds of a feather flock together. Where are the people in my life in just as much pain? When a lighthouse came my way, I lied about how I felt. God will send a lighthouse your way. You won't be able to see them if you are always looking down. To all the lighthouses and prayers that came my way, Thank you. If you are a lighthouse or need a lighthouse, just pray.

"He feels only the pain of his own body, and he mourns only for himself."

Job 14:22

"For I consider that the sufferings of this present time are not worth comparing with the glory that is to be revealed to us."

Romans 8:18

Pray this prayer: *May the words from my mouth and the mediation in my heart be acceptable in thine sight, Oh Lord, AMEN.*

DAY 7 - VICTORY

I woke up with the word victory this morning. It's amazing how some words sound like fire. They get you going. Victory is one of those words. I woke up with chills because of victory. I feel like I hit the lottery. My achievements flash before my eyes when I hear victory. The victory that resonates in my heart is my walk with Christ. God is telling me to invest in myself. I embraced this victory, and I wrote this book. I have victory because God fights all my battles today. Victory takes guts not to fight and just wait on faith to win the war. God taught me that fighting someone else's battle isn't my victory. My younger days were different. I would help my family all the time. I convinced myself they wouldn't have been able to have victory without me. I was a public relations manager telling everyone who crossed my path about their victory. Did I tell you it was because of me? My truth is I had no direction, no plan, and no dreams. For me, victory was anything my money could buy.

It's lunchtime, and I'm on the other side of victory. Fail is the word that's running through my mind. It's so crazy because I carried around other people's successes as well as their failures. I held the weight of the world on my shoulders. How can a little four-letter word have such a significant impact on my life? Gravity always pulls you down. I stayed flat on my back. I looked up and saw no sunlight because my days were always cloudy. I turned on my stomach but didn't have the courage even to do a push-up. I had convinced myself that the fall was greater than the effort to get up. I stayed on the ground until it flattened out. Wow! As I am writing, this just came to me. I just wanted everyone to look the other way so I could get back up. I didn't want anyone to know about my failure. I wanted them to take the blame in my mind. It was all their fault. I was ego-driven and coward tough.

I'm grateful for failure. I have failure daily. It's okay. I have an imaginary ladder on my back for my pitfalls today. I don't see roadblocks. I see hurdles. I will tell you when you have victory. It's when you feel like you no longer have to fight. You don't even care about the outcome. You can trust God with the end result. Faith in God gives me victory to know failure is growth.

"For the LORD your God is he who goes with you to fight for you against your enemies, to give you the victory."

Deuteronomy 20:4

"But thanks be to God, who gives us the victory through our Lord Jesus Christ."

1 Corinthians 15:57

DAY 8 - JOY

Today is a great day. I wake up with joy in my heart. Joy to me is having inner peace and freedom in my mind. It's Saturday; as I sit on a park bench and read a travel magazine, I get so excited, like I'm actually traveling to the places from the pictures. If you don't understand, try this one. I can stand in church and cry. If I still don't get it, keep reading. I don't start over every morning. I wake up climbing higher and higher. Obstacles are coming my way, but more angels are coming to bring me blessings to add joy to my life. My breakfast is chopped inner peace, whole freedom, diced unconditional love, and a godlike liquid to drink.

The biggest challenge I had to process for my joy was my identity. My skin tone was painful growing up. I was always too light for black people and too dark for white people. I didn't know where I fit in. I gave credit for my being in management at 20 years old because of my skin. My curly hair made matters worse. I look at mixed kids and wonder if they feel safe. I didn't have a safe place to go in my mind. If I could go back to the young me and deliver a message, it would be; God is your safety, and he lives. I see mixed kids today and wonder if they struggle with identity. All children deserve to have a safe place to go in their minds.

I want to apologize to all the dark-skinned people I ignored or never met because of my ignorant prejudice. It was never about light or dark, but I made it about that. It is about *GOOD versus EVIL.* I can remember the first time I ate chicken legs and thighs, and I was always told white meat is better than dark. Thighs are juicy, and I prefer them over breast meat today.

I always slept with the light on in my room; it made me feel safe. I now sleep with the light off, which was my first step in trusting God. The darkness makes me still and strengthens my relationship with God. It was the way that I started giving up control and relying on God to guide and protect me.

I can remember the first time I felt the light shining within me. I was paying for my items at the self-checkout, and I got to the question of cash needed back. I usually say no, but that day my spirit said to get $20. I only need money if I'm going out to dinner, and I like to tip with cash instead of on a card. (It is my way of ensuring the server gets the tip.) Some restaurants do group share tips, and I don't think that is fair.

A lady was entering the store with her son. I heard her ask for the change machine. My spirit and I followed them. I walked slowly and let them get started. I reached into my pocket and gave her the $20. It wasn't about my ego; it was about my growth.

Check this out - A light will shine only if there is no darkness.

Is darkness needed to shine a light?

I will dig deeper into light and darkness in my upcoming book-

MY TRUTH: JUST CARE.

I will give you a sneak peek at the thought process. When a thought enters your mind, you must accept it and process it. Accepting it means understanding the thought's motive, consequences, and actions. Process means to decide, act on it, and let it go. I'm going to say that again, let it go. If you let thoughts hang around, they gain the power to have you running laps inside your mind.

"A joyful heart is good medicine, but a crushed spirit dries up the bones."

Proverbs   17:22

"May the God of hope fill you with all joy and peace in believing, so that by the power of the Holy Spirit you may abound in hope."

Romans   15:13

Joy makes me smile for no reason, and the greatest joy I know is that God loves everyone. Although God loves everyone, I'm his favorite because I'm a miracle.

DAY 9 - PRESSURE

I woke up with a headache. The word that comes to mind is pressure, and I immediately start to meditate and relax after taking my morning meds. Pressure doesn't exist in my life today. No one puts pressure on you; you put it on yourself. The only pressure I put on myself is trying to find someone who will accept me being married three times. I tell them upfront when we meet. I don't know why I flip-flop with that part of my past.

Pressure always starts in my mind... like a candle lit with a match.

I pray to God and then unwind ... It blows out then I relax.

I didn't handle pressure when I was a teenager. My life was always in total chaos because of the pressure I conjured up in high school. I remember walking around the grocery store. I got to the aisle with the rat poison. I don't remember the exact pressure I had running around in my mind. It may have been no relationship with my mom or pops; I always felt rejected, desperate, exasperated, or defenseless. The bottom line is the spiritual seeds my grandparents planted dried out. I took the rat poison with a beer that night. I remember waking up. That was the start of many years of trying to figure it out. I was a zombie for the next ten years.

It's a blessing to let God drive the bus today. It allows me to be pressure-free. Risks don't scare me anymore. I know the word is healthy. Risk is one of the words you need to dream. The risk gets greater and greater the more you believe. Risks allow me the passageway to favor with

God. God gives me a favor when I take the risk on him. My confidence is climbing. I must dare myself not to become complacent. Risks keep me hungry and humble at the same time. I have never talked about this risk I took. I remember a risk I took a long time ago. Maybe this risk will help you. I remember going to a family cookout, playing a spades game, talking trash, and drinking. Probably not in that order. I got very drunk. I vaguely remember at least two family members trying to get me to spend the night. I told one yes and slipped into my car. Okay, here it comes. I had my son with me. He was about eight years old. I was so drunk I had to cover one eye to drive home. I was at least 30 miles away. I'm gasping for air typing these words. To my son, please forgive me. Angels got us home that night. My truth is I just have a hangover. I had no remorse. Please, Please, Please, take their keys or call the cops. I could have killed my son as well as myself or someone else. I'm speechless. It's still challenging with a healthy thought process today. I have to recharge my faith every day. I hook up to an endless source of power. God charges my faith in full when I trust him 100%.

"No temptation has overtaken you that is not common to man. God is faithful, and he will not let you be tempted beyond your ability, but with the temptation, he will also provide the way of escape, that you may be able to endure it."

1 Corinthians 10:13

DAY 10 - FOREVER

I woke up this morning thinking about yesterday. I have this guilty feeling of thinking about driving with my son. I started my day in meditation after I took my meds. The first word that comes to mind is forever. I have chills thinking about the 2nd and 3rd chances I've been given. Thank you, Lord. What are the qualifications to be mine forever? I only have two. Love God and be yourself. My future is so bright it blinds my eyes. God keeps me planted right here, right now. Staying in the moment allows me to remain humble. I used to struggle with looking up at the mountains. God allows me to see over the mountains. I put all my faith in him. It doesn't matter what's on the other side. I know that if I did things my way, I would screw it up. There should be an I in ego. It should be spelled "eiego". The ego can be a driving force, it can drive you to be the best and push you to the top, or the ego can mislead you into diving off a cliff.

Here is just a question I want to throw out there. How much of your brain do you actually use?

How much of your brain can you actually use?

I don't know; I was just asking. I might write a book on it after doing the research.

Where I'm going with this?

I am going to God.

God is the creator, and the Bible is God's word; it is a book of a way to live. It may start boring, but stay with it.

The part of your brain that tells you it is boring is evil, and the evil wants you to give up.

Every morning I make a gratitude list. I've broken my rearview and side-view mirrors. The past is history. Enjoying the moment makes me thankful. Thankful for knowing what God has for me is for me. God sends angels my way every day. I can see them looking through the goggles of blood that was shed on the cross. I can forgive myself daily. God has already forgiven me.

The seed God planted in me has always been there. It only began to grow when I gave it water and fertilizer. Faith in God is the water, and growth is the fertilizer. I wrote this book in 14 hours. I already have six books written within a year. I sit down and still tremble today, and all the glory goes to God. I am grateful for the gifts he has given me. I'm prepared for those who think this isn't my gift. If the ink on these pages can save one person from evil, I'm paid in full. Today is a typical day for me. I may start my day off struggling, but I have a healthy thought process with myself. The struggle doesn't last long.

Every morning He speaks to me. The hardest part was learning to listen.

"My grace is sufficient for you, for my power is made perfect in weakness." "Therefore I will boast all the more gladly of my weakness, so that the power of Christ may rest upon me. For the sake of Christ, then, I am content with weaknesses, insults, hardships, persecutions, and calamities. For when I am weak, then I am strong."

2 Corinthians 12:9-10

CLOSURE

I'm trying to come up with a word to explain my life today - I got it. The word is healthy. The first four letters are H...E...A...L. I was always in the middle of a storm. My life was chaos and confusion. I brought it on myself but never took ownership. My normal was unhealthy. This journal started as a way to vent. It has salvaged my life. I dated myself for the first time in my life by doing this 10-Day, 10-Word challenge. I didn't just look at myself as negative or positive. I looked at my feeling. I became emotionally attached to my daily word. I didn't realize my emotions had blocked the feeling I needed and built walls with other feelings that kept me isolated in my mind.

Because of my childhood, trust was a very emotional word for me. I never trusted anyone. Today, I realize I never trusted myself. I expected happiness from others, and I didn't trust them when they let me down. I developed a learned behavior not to deal with feelings that were uncomfortable, and it allowed me to stuff and hide problems without a solution.

Today, I don't wait on the storm to pass. I open the door and walk out in the rain. The rain beating on my face doesn't cause pain anymore; it's cool and therapeutic today. The problems I work through are calm because I have closure. I don't have any more bad days. I stay honest with myself, process my thoughts, and let God drive the bus.

I know I said I would wait and talk about my thought process in my upcoming book. I have to say this. When a thought enters your mind, you must accept it and process it. Accepting it means understanding the motive, consequences, and actions. Process means to decide, act on it, and let it go. I'm so grateful for a healthy thought process today. This 10-Day, 10-Word challenge taught me something priceless. I had deep-rooted scars with words like sex, mom, brother, sister, and so many more. Doing my daily routine, these words would take me back down memory lane. It's crazy because I still wonder how my mind works when I sleep. I wake up sometimes with thoughts from the day before.

Today I find closure in understanding that some words will have pain attached to them. It's okay - I process them and let them go. Letting them go is understanding words like pain are good for you, and they make you appreciate the sunshine even better. I want to close with your relationship with God.

I remember standing out in the middle of a thunderstorm with a loud burst of lighting. It doesn't matter what you said to me; I wouldn't hear you. It's hard for me not to give God all the glory for my life today. I had complete control of my life, and It was a whole mess. Looking deep within myself was easier than the first step. I took the first step only because of desperation - I had no reason to live.

I woke up one morning thinking about marriage and heard a voice say to write about it. I grabbed a piece of paper and began to write. My first ten days are inked out for you; the rest is history. I want to thank you for allowing me to share my experience with you.

It may not be your story or your journey, and we may not have anything in common, but I do know one thing; to dream, you must be free. To be free, you must have inner peace. To have inner peace, you must have faith. Having faith makes it easy to dream.

Now go get yours.

Thank you.

"For by grace you have been saved through faith. And this is not your own doing: it is the gift of God."

Ephesians 2:8

SHOWTIME

Now it is your turn to start a 10-word, 10-day journey to see how it can begin to transform your life. Write down the first word that comes to mind each morning when you wake up. Unleash the word on paper. If you have no time to process that word right then, you can come back to it later in the day. Just make sure you write that word down. It's the word God put on your heart, and you don't want to forget it.

A journal is your safe place. It is a place where you can identify and process your state of mind, where you are right here and right now.

When a thought enters your mind, you must accept it and process it. Accepting it means understanding the thought's motive, consequences, and actions. Processing it means deciding, acting on it, and letting it go. I'm going to say it again- let it go. If you let thoughts hang around, they gain the power to have you running laps inside your mind.

If you have years hiding away in your mind. It will take time and hard work to process the emotions and thoughts accompanying that day's word. Take the time and energy to gain closure of those emotions and feelings so that you can open your heart and mind to bigger and better things that God has in store for you.

Take the 10-days, 10-words journey to unlock your mind and dream. There is a seed planted inside you, begging for water and fertilizer. On this 10-day journey, you will feel empowered and free; embrace it.

> *"May the God of hope fill you with all joy and peace in believing, so that by the power of the Holy Spirit you may abound in hope."*
>
> *Romans 15:13*

It's so easy to look at others, but it is hard to look at yourself honestly and graciously. But now it is your turn to make YOUR dreams come true. You can do it with one word, one day at a time. At the end of the day, you will have closure, the closure you need to clear the room. You will clear space in your heart and mind to fill it with all the good you deserve.

Take this 10 DAY, 10 WORD
challenge and set yourself free.

Start in your own journal, or get my 30-Day Journal that inspires and motivates you daily. It's hard to start, but once you begin to feel free and lighter, with less baggage, you will want to continue as I did. The more days that went by, the freer I felt. The 30-Day Journal allows you to keep going.

KEEP GOING

I wanted to continue with the next ten days to share my progress as I continued to write in my journal. Know that your journal is your safe place to write down your feelings and how you feel about those feelings. Taking ownership of your thoughts and feelings takes courage; if I can do it, so can you. I want you to learn a new behavior on how to process thoughts. I believe when a thought enters your mind, you must accept it and process it. Accepting it means understanding the thought's motive, consequences, and actions. Process means to decide, act on it, and let it go. In other words, just write what comes to mind and start processing your emotions and feelings inside you. Once you start processing those emotions and feelings holding you back, you will begin to feel free. Once you feel free, you will be able to dream. When you start dreaming, you can start fulfilling your dreams and living your best life. You may be in a good place in your life. Let's take it to higher ground, continuing to journal.

Journaling is the best way to start processing thoughts, so start writing. Write in your own journal or begin using the My Truth 30-Day Journal to start your 10-day, 10-words. I know you will want to keep going as I did, feeling better and freer every day. This 30-Day Journal contains inspirational sayings, phrases, quotes, and tips to get you through those tough days when you get stuck or don't feel like you are making progress.

"Do not be afraid; you will not be put to shame. Do not fear disgrace; you will not be humiliated. You will forget the shame of your youth and remember no more the reproach of your widowhood."

Isaiah   54:4   NIV

LOST

I woke up with the word lost in my mind, not physically but emotionally and mentally lost. I can tell you the physical address I woke up from and the time on the clock. Lost has many definitions; one is defined as no longer to be found, possessed, or retained. Lost can also mean something someone has failed to win. I am using the definition of having gone astray, bewildered as to place or missed the way.

This feeling of missing the way or going astray comes without a heartbeat. I feel drained and want to close my eyes and go back to sleep. This feeling makes me want to give up. What do I do?

Picture this; a "lost and found" box. This is how I envision this feeling today. People lose stuff at work or shopping in a store. I left my phone on a shelf at the grocery store. It never made it to the lost and found box. I had to get another phone. That pissed me off. OK, I'm back on track. Thanks for listening. This box reminds me of this feeling. I imprisoned myself in my mind to stay lost. I would stuff my feelings inside with no way out. I now know the box has two words on it. I always looked at the lost part of the phrase and accepted it. The lost is the problem, but the found is the solution. Finding God allows me to accept how I'm feeling. I fall to my knees and pray for understanding. Every day isn't going to start with a bang. Every day isn't going to be smooth sailing. Having a healthy thought process keeps me grounded. I start thanking God with a gratitude list. The L, the O, the S, and the T leave me like it never existed.

"My people hath been lost sheep: their shepherds have caused them to go astray, they have turned them away on the mountains: they have gone from mountain to hill, they have forgotten their resting place."

Jeremiah 50:6 KJV

I often wonder about the attack of resentments while you are asleep. Resentments are feelings of displeasure at a remark, person, or act causing insult. Resentments do many things in your mind to create havoc and chaos. Resentments take up space in your mind. Resentments move in and grow thick walls. Resentments build a condominium in your mind. I use the word condominium, not an apartment, because resentments are territorial taking ownership. Resentments have no maximum value or expiration date. Pain and anger provide room service for resentments. Pain is a terrifying emotion. It only attacks you when you are down and want to pull you deeper into a self-made pit.

My journal has allowed me to understand I was only seeing the mess. God allows me to look for miracles through his works in my life. God sends angels my way with direction signals. I see and feel them today. I stop at the market on my way home. I get in line with three people ahead of me. The cashier is complaining left and right. She was saying her feet hurt, and she was hungry, along with where did all these people come from?

I started praying for God to guide my thoughts. It's my turn at the register, and I look to the right. What do you think I saw?

Come on, one guess!

Exactly...It was a *Lost and Found* box. I began to smile. I looked into her eyes and told her God is amazing. I asked her if she had attended church. She said, "no", so I gave her some recommendations. The lady was smiling when I left. My day started lost and ended with someone else possibly being found. Today was a great day!

"But if our gospel is hid, it is hid to them that are lost:"
2 Corinthians 4:3 KJV

HUMBLE

This morning, I woke up with the word humble. Wow, I love this feeling. I'm very in tune with my emotions now, and I believe there are no good or bad feelings, and I process the good and bad feelings the same. I think being too high can crack the back door for your ego to sneak in, so I make my gratitude list. I thank God for those blessings that make me feel so good inside.

Humility, to me, is that warm and fuzzy feeling. It's not caring who's wrong or right. It's knowing God already knows the outcome. I trust God and enjoy each moment. I know during the day, I will be tested. I pack a whole humble pie. I don't care what others think of me. I only care what God thinks about me. It's not about how others treat me but how I treat them.

I say this prayer daily:

"May the words from my mouth and mediation in my heart be acceptable in thy sight, Oh Lord," I call this my humble pie prayer.

Humility can sometimes attack you like a double-edged sword. It makes you feel like you're being disrespected sometimes. I remind myself it's not about me. It's about **good vs. evil**. The evil spirit will try to do anything to get you out of character. One thing people say is to accept a person because of the way they are. I say pray for them more than yourself. Don't accept negative people. When prayers go up, blessings come down. I stop to get gas on the way home. I pay at the pump. I go inside to buy some water. The attendant tells me I must spend $5 to use my card. I started looking around. The person behind me in line said, "No problem, I got it." I tell him thank you. Sometimes to stay humble, you must be humbled. I'm so humbled for my thought process today. I'm so humbled with my journal. Thank you, Lord.

"For if anyone thinks he is something, when he is nothing, he deceives himself. "

Galatians 6:3

"The reward for humility and fear of the LORD is riches and honor and life."

Proverbs 22:4

"When pride comes, then comes disgrace, but with the humble comes wisdom."

Proverbs 11:2

FATHER

Today, my word is father. This word has a double meaning for me. I will start with my birth father. My father was always bigger than life to me as a child. My brother and sister were needier than I was, and I didn't want attention, but I now know it was needed. The word that comes to mind is validation.

Validation matters from people you care about. I didn't understand validation was needed until I got older. Let's define validation using the dictionary; the act of confirming something is true or correct. That's not the one. The act of legally or officially certifying or approving something. Not this one, either. The act of affirming a person, feelings, ideas, and actions as acceptable and worthy. Bingo. My father never told me he loved me. My father never saw me play sports. I couldn't tell you my father's favorite color or food—his likes or dislikes. I would even bet my life he didn't know mine either. I had this discussion about a year ago with a friend of mine. She told me to grow up and get over it. You are an adult now. I have talked about resentments. People rent space in your mind and don't even know it.

The only way to kick them out is to process the feeling. Once again, my thought process is accepting it and processing it. Accepting it means understanding the thought's motive, consequences, and actions. Process means to decide, act on it, and let it go. I was stuck out of the gate and didn't accept anything because I didn't understand.

Now, I have accepted it because of my kids. My kids are with two different mothers, and I'm blessed they got along growing up. My dad, with his new family, always made me feel like an outsider. I didn't belong. I held on to the feeling for so long because I didn't understand why he didn't fight for me. Children and teenagers should always have a safe place to go in their minds when alone. I don't know if I'm a better father, but I tore down the walls that had me isolated.

My father passed on August 16, 2009. My job allows me to be around engineers. They remind me of my father. I forgave him a long time ago. The hard part was to forget. I wish I had had a healthy thought process 40 years ago. I talk to my father at least 3 or 4 times a week. Today he lives in my heart. I only care about right here, right now. Herman Matthew Wiley Currence Jr, I love you, POPS. I know you can hear me. I can finally hear you. Thank you for being my father. *REST IN PEACE.*

I want to start off with a story about my daughter. I was spending the weekend with my daughter. Her alarm goes off. I can hear it. It's one of those electronic play toys this younger generation has. The alarm starts talking, "Good Morning, Latoya. You are beautiful. You are going to have an amazing day. Your father loves you." I got up later and chopped it up with her. I told her her alarm humbled me. Are you ready for this? I'm waiting on the alarm to go off the following day. The alarm goes off; "Good morning Latoya. You are beautiful. You are going to have an amazing day. Your heavenly father loves you." OMG, I couldn't stop laughing at myself. I'm so proud of Latoya's relationship with God. We laughed so hard when she got up. I still laugh today when I think about it.

I want to talk about my relationship with my heavenly father. I had lost hope for happiness. I had lost hope for inner peace. I didn't have a safe place to go in my mind when I was alone. My way wasn't working. Out of desperation, I began to pray. I don't remember my first prayer. I do remember the first time I felt an angel God sent my way. I was single for five years. I went on my first date. It was an online date. The lady went to the bathroom. I grabbed a napkin and wrote a poem. She came back. I read it to her. She told me she was an author. She had self-published a book. She kept pushing me. We only dated for two months. I sat down to write for the first time. I trembled. It was an out-of-body experience. It is still like that even today.

I joke about never writing a book. I hear angels whispering in my ears. The more I write, the closer I get to God. God sent me another angel. One of my colleagues. He loves the Lord. He kept telling me every time I saw for me to read my Bible. One year later, I did. It is so therapeutic to get up every morning and have that time with God. It motivates me to share my experience with others to read the Bible. I'm trying to tell you that God has always been with me. God has always sent angels my way. Accepting God allows you to see them. God will give you goggles to see miracles. The biggest miracle you will see is yourself. You will be able to look in the mirror, not at it. God validates me that I matter. Believing in God has taken my confidence to unstoppable heights. I know God officially certified me. My life today is amazing. I have a question, "Do you feel you are worthy of being in the presence of God?" I promise that it will be revealed if you honestly continue to journal.

"Honor your father and mother, that your days be long in the land the LORD your God is giving you."

Exodus 20:12

"Hear, ye children, the instruction of a father, and attend to know understanding."

Proverbs 4:1 KJV

GOD

I woke up with the word God this morning. I can hear my mom saying, "God is real, and He lives."

One of the reasons I love my job is I get to be in contact with people one on one daily. It allows me to talk about God. My outlook on life changed drastically when I put God in control. To end on a good note, I will start with how my life was before Christ.

I started most of my mornings with a *just because* attitude. I had to get up*, just because*. I went to work *just because*. Everything was *just because.* I never took ownership of any mistakes. I was ego-tough and coward driven. I loved myself on the outside, and I cried alone on the inside.

Resentments had built a high-rise building in my mind. I got on the elevator daily, from my past, with daily insults that gave me a reason to have a pity party. I would only hear people saying negative things, and it was like gasoline on a fire. Negativity would get me to the elevator, and I would go up and down memory lane. One thing that would quieten the chatter was the feeling of intoxication.

Being inebriated was greater than any resentments I had. A good cold beer would make me forget about everything. Looking back, I would try to find a reason to get pissed off so I could justify wanting a cold beer. One word to describe my life before Christ was messy. Messy means causing a mess, embarrassing, difficult, or unpleasant. I was a very messy person.

Now, I start every morning excited; today was no different because God loves me.

God's love allows me to make mistakes. The mistakes today are battle scars, and they remind me of making it through because of God's grace and mercy. Love is the only feeling that can overpower anger, pain, hate, fear, and you know the last one - Yes, RESENTMENTS. Love tore down the high-rise building in my mind immediately, and I gave God the same unconditional love he gave me.

The negativity left the same day. I hear people talk today. I try to tell them something positive, so I share my experience with God. The feeling is better than any beer I have ever drank. I don't have to go to the store. I don't need any money. I can plug into an endless source of power. The power of God has empowered me to love myself inside out.

I'm not messy anymore. I'm a miracle. More words that also come to mind are marvel, wonder, rarity, or phenomenon. I have inner peace because of God. I have freedom in my mind because of God. I don't have to make any decisions because of God. I just sit back and ride. The level of trust and love will grow. Trust is the water, and love is the fertilizer. You can grow anything with these. I'm still under construction. God only puts on me what I can bear. I no longer feel like I have to carry things on my back. God has my back, and it's the best feeling in the world. Now is a good time to get everything off your back.

"God is real, and He lives."

"Let the morning bring me word of your unfailing love, for I have put my trust in you. Show me the way I should go, for to you I entrust my life."

Psalm 143:8 NIV

"For God gave us a spirit not of fear but power and love and self-control."

2 Timothy 1:7

COMPROMISE

I woke up with the word compromise in my mind. I can feel my growth on this journey. My thoughts have become more thoughtful. Compromise is a cool-sounding word. It carries a lot of weight. Off the top of my head, I would say it is 50/50. I know some of my compromising agreements aren't 50/50, and I'm OK with that. I wanted it to be 90/10 in my past because I always wanted things to go my way. If something didn't work out, I would say you had the 90%. My compromise today isn't about numbers. It's about understanding God drives the bus. I trust him with the percentages. God reminds me that He gave me two ears and one mouth; to shut my mouth and listen. I can be very quick to draw conclusions without hearing the whole scenario.

Compromise doesn't happen without two-way communication. I have learned how to act and not to react. I will ask questions or get clarification on something just to ensure that I understand. You would think everybody would do that, but I know that takes effort.

Compromise is a learned behavior. It's not about winning or losing some battles; it's about the war—the war of life.

How do you win?

Just let God fight your battles.

"Know this, my beloved brothers: let every person be quick to hear, slow to speak, slow to anger;"

James   1:19

"Let no corrupting talk come out of your mouths, but only such as is good for building up, as fits occasion, that it may give grace to those who hear."

Ephesians   4:29

"Set a guard, O LORD, over my mouth; keep watch over the door of my lips!"

Psalm   141:3

HUNGRY

I woke up with the word hungry this morning. All my life, this word was defined as wanting food, and I know now my hunger is a desire for more. I hunger for more understanding of the Bible. I hunger for more knowledge of God. I hunger for more understanding of my purpose in life.

I read the Bible most mornings. Sometimes later in the day. I get stuck on some bible verses for days. I pray to God for understanding, the understanding of how it fits into my life. I have to pay attention because God always sends messages to help me understand. I have to get out of my own way sometimes. It is so simple. Just have enough faith of a mustard seed.

I'm writing another book along with this one. It's called; *THE HOMELESS: DRUG ADDICTION, MENTAL ILLNESS, MOTHERHOOD, OR SURVIVAL.*

As I've been researching homelessness, I thought some of these people were scary, and I wasn't sure how to act, feel or think about it. I was reading in the book of Matthew one morning and was led to this verse.

"For I was hungry and you gave me food, I was thirsty and you gave me drink, I was a stranger and you welcomed me."

Matthew   25:35

As I was looking at this scripture, I stopped and pondered...

Am I supposed to let my window down at the stop light?

Am I supposed to give money regardless?

And then this is what happened to me that day when I had so many questions about what I was supposed to do. I was in a big box store line, and the lady in the line in front of me said, "I forgot something." As I waited for about five minutes, I told the cashier I would pay for her things, so the cashier started ringing up my items as the lady returned. Frazzled, the lady looked me in the eyes and said, "I'm sorry you had to wait. My daughter lost her first child due to a miscarriage, and I can only imagine what she is feeling", as she handed the cashier her item. When the cashier told her that I was paying for her things, the lady thanked me, hugged me, and told the cashier that I was her angel. I told her I would pray for her and her daughter and that God answered my prayers too.

I was looking for someone who needed something that I could provide. God provided for that family through me as He answered my questions from the scriptures I read that morning. On my ride home, I thanked God left and right as I smiled, laughed, and cried the whole way home. I have never lost a child, and I couldn't imagine what the lady's daughter was going through.

Feeling blessed about never going through the loss of a child, I was blessing someone in a way that God wanted. God will let us know when it is our turn to be a blessing to someone in need. We just have to stop and listen once in a while.

And my God will supply every need of yours according to his riches in glory in Christ Jesus.

Philippians 4:19 ESV

Jesus said to them, "I am the bread of life; whoever comes to me shall not hunger, and whoever believes in me shall never thirst."

John 6:35

"But he answered, "It is written," Man shall not live by bread alone, but by every word that comes from the mouth of God."

Matthew 4:4

You are not alone; God is right there with you. It comes in many different forms, but He will provide. It says so right there in the scriptures!

LISTEN

Listen. Listen to what? I close my eyes. I hear a car horn, my alarm going off. I need to dig deeper. Listening has changed my life so much. I would stand right in front of people and not listen to a word they said. I was so preoccupied in my mind with nonsense.

My listening skills began when I started journaling. I was able to listen to my own voice, and it slowed me down. I sometimes wonder whether people listen to me or not, or do they even know the meaning of the word listen? Although most people use their ears to hear things, not all know how to listen or actually hear what a person is saying to them. To actively listen to someone is a learned behavior.

To listen is defined in the dictionary as a verb, as paying attention with the ear, with hearing.

Did you know that?

How about hear?

To hear is a verb defined in the dictionary as to perceive with the ear.

Did you know that?

My definition of listening today is hearing with undivided attention. I have listened to music all my life; today, I enjoy listening to gospel music, and I can block out all other sounds to hear my song. I've learned how to apply this when listening to people. My kids tell me to respond with words like yes, OK, good, or wow. This helps the other person believe you are listening.

Now let's look at the word hear. I believe it has a more substantial meaning. It means understanding what the person is saying. Not only do you need to listen to what the person says, but you also need to hear them. So for me hearing them means that I understand and am committed.

So when speaking with my kids today, I will say,

"Did you hear what I was saying?"

"Do you understand?"

"But when I speak with you, I will open your mouth, and you shall say to them, 'Thus says the Lord God.' He who will hear, let him hear; and he who will refuse to hear, let him refuse, for they are a rebellious house."
                                        Ezekiel 3:27

"Let the wise hear and increase in learning, and the one who understands obtain guidance,"
                                        Proverbs   1:5

"So faith comes from hearing, and hearing through the word of Christ."
                                        Romans   10:17

END

I woke up with the word, end. I think of the end of a movie—the end of a good book. Another thing I think about for the word end is death. My grandmother was murdered on November 22, 1986. I was so mad at God for taking my grandmother away from me, and I walked away with a big chip on my shoulder. I only had two emotions. They were angry and sad.

What was wrong?

Keep reading, I'll tell you.

In my past, the end meant the relationship was over. Some I didn't end. The end always made me play the what-if game. What did I do wrong? What do I change with my next? What if she wants me back? The end is the beginning of your next life experience with closure. The biggest thing I didn't learn about ending, death, and relationships was closure. Today, the end is closure. My grandmother is a place I'm striving to be. My relationships were over because I was spiritually broken. You will never heal if you don't have a healthy thought process. What are the first four letters in healthy? H E A L How do I do it? Glad you asked. My thought process is simple. When a thought enters your mind, you must accept it and process it. Accepting it means understanding the thought's motive, consequences, and actions. Process means to decide, act on it, and let it go. Let it go. The more you do it, the easier it gets. You can do this. LET IT GO.

"For God so loved the world, that he gave his only Son, that whoever believes in him should not perish but have eternal life. For God did not send his Son into the world to condemn the world, but in order that the world might be saved through him."

John   3:16-17

"But the one who endures to the end will be saved."

Matthew   24:13

HOPE

Hope is a heartfelt word to me. I know what it feels like not to have hope. I know what it feels like not to have a reason to want to live. I will try to remember as it seems so long ago. I felt like I was on an amusement ride. It was going round and round, up and down, and it would never stop. The older I got, the faster it went. I would pass people outside the ride. There were places I wanted to get off. I tried to jump off but didn't have the courage. I fall to my knees and pray for understanding out of desperation. Now that was the easy part. I had to get back off the ride and go in reverse. This time I stopped when I saw the people. I had to forgive them. People only treat you the way you allow yourself to be treated. My normal was pain. I stopped at places that caused me pain. I let it go. I stopped at events that bought a condo in my mind. I process them. I forgot about them. They were my past. Your past isn't where you came from but what you went through. You made it. Move on; let it go. So now I have hope.

What is hope? Hope can be a noun and a verb. A noun version is a feeling of what can be for the best. A verb version is to desire, believe or trust. I have a bible verse that won't leave me.

"Now faith is the assurance of things hoped for, the conviction of things not seen."

Hebrews   11:1

Even today, I remind myself that I'm human. I sometimes only see the mess. God reminds me of the miracle. I want to close with the miracles in your life. Don't get caught up in the miracles. Don't forget about the miracle worker. I feed my spirit during the day. It's easy to thank God for answering your prayers. How often to thank him for the good times? Thanking God for the good times has allowed me to have a gratitude list every morning. Just like there are no good and bad emotions, there are no good or bad blessings. Things may not turn out as you want, but God knows the outcome. Keep hope in the miracle worker you won't see with your eyes. God might not show up when you want him, but he will be there right on time.

"For by grace you have been saved through faith. And this is not your own doing; it is the gift of God, not a result of works, so that no one may boast."

Ephesians 2:8-9

JOURNAL

A journal is a safe place to write down your feeling, emotions, and things that come into your mind. It is where you can identify and process where you are right now in your life. If you have years of hiding in your mind, that's fine. My testimony is my truth, and you will create your testimony to be your truth. You must be honest with yourself and be ready for change.

If you are in a good place but stuck, then it will help you progress forward. Take *Ten Days, Ten Words* to unlock your mind to dream. There is a seed planted inside you begging for water and fertilizer. You will, on this ten-day journey, feel more empowered. Feeling empowered will take you further than you can imagine.

Once you complete the Ten Days, Ten Words journal challenge, you can use the My Truth Journal that continues for as long as you feel the need, using the same technique. Using this technique will bring up more feelings and emotions than you thought. While this may happen, you will be able to set free what has been holding you back from fulfilling your dreams and living your life to the fullest.

How hard is it to wake up and write a word down? I think it is hard because it takes courage to look at yourself. Do you know that most people look at other people more than themselves? That can change. Enjoy your journey of becoming free to dream.

Dreams do come true!

ABOUT THE AUTHOR

Dwight Hairston Currence resides in Charlotte, North Carolina. He loves the Lord and strives daily to inspire others to be confident in who they are. Dwight desires everyone to understand how wonderful life can be when you simply love God first and learn to accept who you truly are.